June Fischer

RUTH WEBB LEE'S HANDBOOK

MAGNET AND GRAPE WINE JUG

RUTH WEBB LEE'S
HANDBOOK

OF EARLY AMERICAN
PRESSED GLASS PATTERNS

RUTH WEBB LEE   PUBLISHER

FRAMINGHAM CENTRE - - MASSACHUSETTS

SEVENTH PRINTING

IN EXPLANATION

It is not so many years ago that collectors of American blown glass and writers on the subject attached little importance to the later commercial glassware which flooded our markets during the decades immediately preceding and following the Civil War. Collectors of rarities found no pleasure in acquiring anything so plentiful as glass made in America from 1840 to 1890. But the urge to buy essentially American antiques grew stronger year by year, and with it a more intelligent view of the desirability of securing what would harmonize with furnishings that would create an entirely American atmosphere in the dining-room. Today discriminating collectors are as keenly interested in matching sets of this popular glass, both crystal and colored, as they used to be in acquiring the rare forms of blown glass.

Popular demand necessitated a standard nomenclature for early American pressed glass. It was a source of annoyance and expense to both collectors and dealers to find that different sections of the country had different names for the same pattern. No collector could be certain that if he ordered Baltimore pear from Ohio he would receive what Pennsylvania or Connecticut dealers knew by that name. But even worse was the fact that many attractive patterns were practically uncollectible by mail because they had no name at all. Descriptions and rubbings did not always prove successful in obtaining matched specimens for the amateur who wanted to complete a set of the pattern of which the trade name had been lost and no substitute agreed upon.

Realizing the urgent need of a common language on the subject decided me to attempt what had been declared by some editors and writers to be an impossible feat; namely, to classify

In Explanation

the myriad designs of glass produced in a highly commercialized era; that is, from 1840 through the '70's and '80's.

Early American Pressed Glass was released to an eager group of glass lovers in December 1931. From the first collectors and dealers, as well as librarians, accepted the book as the standard authority. It established once for all a nomenclature and it gave the first accurate classification of the hundreds of patterns and forms that are collectible.

Only a pioneer book on a given subject can bring to light material which was unobtainable at the time the manuscript was written. Letters from interested readers poured in and resulting research brought out a large number of old trade catalogues, thereby affording information on when, where and by whom many of our popular designs were made. As a result of these valuable discoveries, it was deemed advisable to revise and enlarge *Early American Pressed Glass*. This revised edition was published in December 1933. The book is now in its twelfth large printing.

The constantly increasing sales of *Early American Pressed Glass* eight years after its initial appearance indicate no abatement in the demand for accurate information on the part of an ever-growing horde of collectors. These same collectors, as well as countless dealers, asked for sets of the photographs and line drawings used in my book, to carry with them on their travels. *Early American Pressed Glass,* with its 712 pages, is too heavy to take about handily. It is therefore the purpose of this Handbook to serve as an indispensable guide to old pattern glass, affording means of identifying patterns, alike to dealers and collectors on collecting trips as well as to those who do not own *Early American Pressed Glass*.

RUTH WEBB LEE

Framingham Centre,
Massachusetts.

PLATE 1—GOBLETS

Ashburton	Loop
Flute	Excelsior

PLATE 2—GOBLETS

Colonial   Crystal
Argus   Mirror

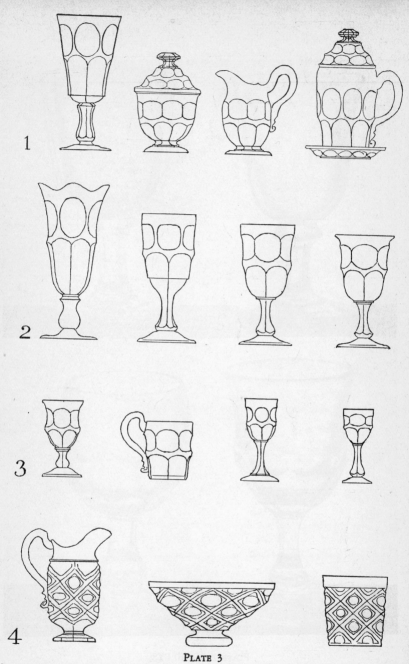

PLATE 3

1. ASHBURTON celery vase, sugar bowl, creamer, toddy glass with plate.
2. ASHBURTON celery vase, goblet with disconnected ovals, goblet in usual form, goblet with flaring bowl.
3. ASHBURTON egg cup, handled cup, wine, cordial.
4. DIAMOND THUMBPRINT creamer, bowl with low foot, tumbler.

PLATE 4

1. EXCELSIOR goblet, footed tumbler, double egg cup, egg cup.
2. EXCELSIOR tumbler, wine, cordial, claret.
3. LOOP covered compote on high standard, deep plate, covered bowl.
4. PETAL and LOOP open compote, sugar bowl, bowl of sauce dish.

M'KEE & BROTHERS,

FLINT GLASS MANUFACTURERS, PITTSBURGH, PA.

Eugenie Celery.

Eugenie Sugar.

Eugenie Goblet.

½ pt. Eugenie Footed Tumbler.

Eugenie Champagne.

Eugenie Wine.

9 in. Eugenie Footed Dish and Cover.

Eugenie Cordial.

Eugenie Egg.

7 in. Eugenie Footed Dish and Cover.

PLATE 5—EUGENIE PATTERN

Reproduced directly from page of old trade catalogue, M'Kee & Brothers, Pittsburgh, Pa.

M'KEE & BROTHERS,

FLINT GLASS MANUFACTURERS, PITTSBURGH, PA.

Eureka Goblet.

Eureka Pt. Tumbler.

Eureka Champagne.

Eureka Wine.

Eureka Egg.

Eureka Cordial.

4 in. Eureka Nappy.

6 in. Eureka Nappy.

7 in. Eureka Dish.

8 in. Eureka Dish.

9 in. Eureka Dish.

6 in. Eureka Sweetmeat and Cover.

6 in. Eureka Footed Nappy and Cover.

6 in. Eureka Nappy and Cover.

PLATE 6—EUREKA PATTERN

Reproduced directly from page of old trade catalogue M'Kee & Brothers, Pittsburgh, Pa.

M'KEE & BROTHERS,

FLINT GLASS MANUFACTURERS, PITTSBURGH, PA.

Pt. Ex. Decanter.

Pt. Ex. Pitcher.

Ex. Ale.

Ex. Bitter.

½ qt. Ex. foot Tumb.

¼ qt. Ex. Ship Tumb.

10 in. Ex. Bowl.

Qt. Ex. Decanter.

Qt. Ex. Pitcher.

PLATE 7—EXCELSIOR PATTERN

Reproduced directly from page of old trade catalogue, M'Kee & Brothers, Pittsburgh, Pa.

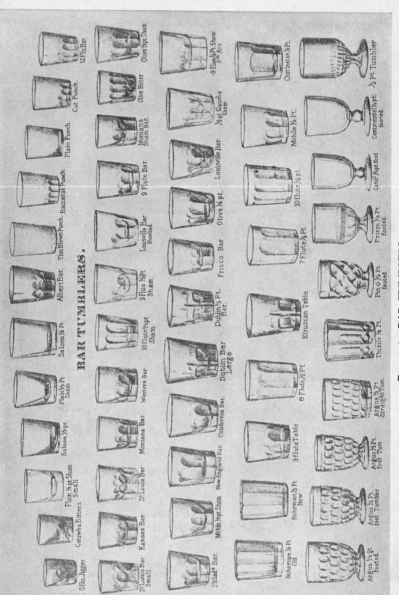

BAR TUMBLERS.

PLATE 8—BAR TUMBLERS

Reproduced directly from page of old trade catalogue, Bakewell, Pears & Co. Pittsburgh, Pa.

M'KEE & BROTHERS,

Flint Glass Manufacturers, Pittsburgh, Pa

10 in. Crystal Bowl.

Crystal Spoon Holder

Crystal Cream.

Crystal Ale.

Qt. Crystal Pitcher.

8 in. Crystal Dish, footed, and Cover.

Crystal Celery.

8 in. Crystal Bowl.

Crystal Sugar.

PLATE 9—CRYSTAL PATTERN

Reproduced directly from page of old trade catalogue, M'Kee & Brothers, Pittsburgh, Pa.

M'KEE & BROTHERS,

Flint Glass Manufacturers, Pittsburgh, Pa.

8 in. Cracker Bowl.

6 in. Crystal Nappy and Cover.

6 in. Crystal Sugar Bowl & Cover.

Qt. Crystal Decanter.

10 in. Cracker Bowl.

Crystal Goblet. Crystal Champagne. Crystal Wine. Crystal Egg. ½ pt. Crystal Tum. ½ pt. Crystal Bar Tum. Gill Crystal Bar Tum.

PLATE 9A—CRYSTAL PATTERN

Reproduced directly from page of old trade catalogue. M'Kee & Brothers, Pittsburgh, Pa.

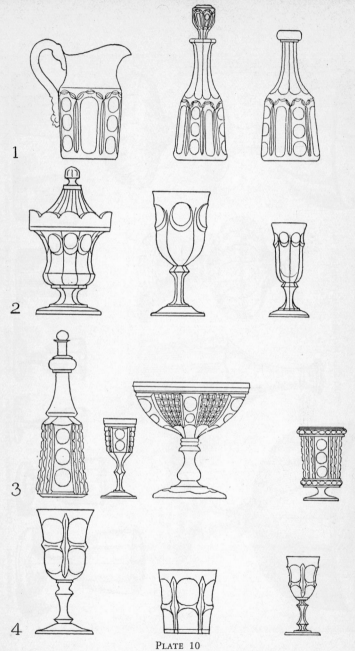

PLATE 10

1. WASHINGTON water pitcher, decanter with original stopper, decanter with bar lip.
2. COLONIAL sugar bowl, goblet, ale glass.
3. WAFFLE and THUMBPRINT decanter with patent stopper, cordial, compote, spoonholder.
4. BIGLER goblet, tumbler, cordial.

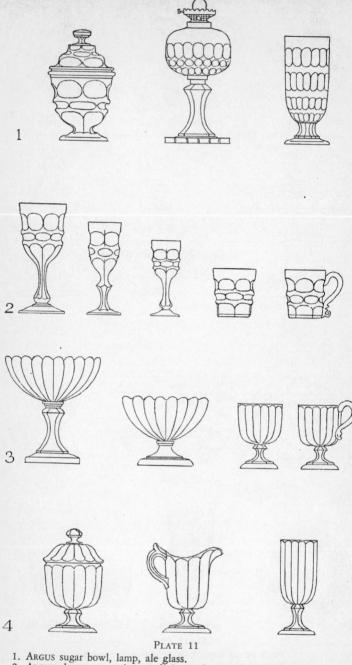

PLATE 11

1. ARGUS sugar bowl, lamp, ale glass.
2. ARGUS champagne, wine, cordial, whiskey tumbler, handled cup.
3. HUBER compote on high standard, compote on low foot, egg cup, handled custard.
4. HUBER sugar bowl, creamer, celery vase.

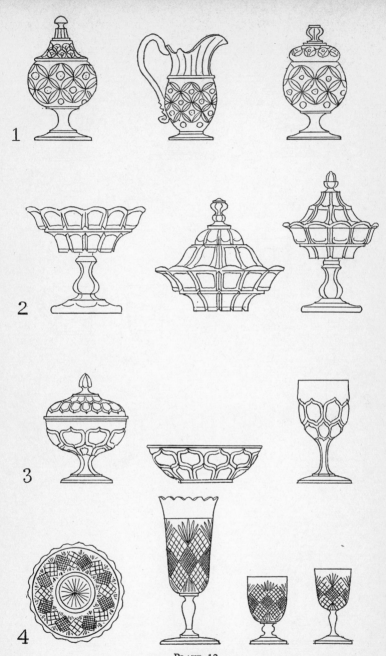

PLATE 12

1. **FOUR PETAL** sugar bowl, creamer, sugar bowl.
2. **PRESSED BLOCK** compote, covered bowl, compote.
3. **OVAL MITRE** compote, oval dish, goblet.
4. **SUNBURST** plate, celery vase, egg cup, wine glass.

PLATE 13

1. BLAZE goblet, sugar bowl, creamer, spoonholder.
2. STEDMAN decanter with bar lip, syrup pitcher, goblet, egg cup, cordial
3. PRISM decanter with bar lip, water pitcher, goblet, egg cup, cordial.
4. FLUTE syrup jug, goblet, champagne, wine.

PLATE 14

1. SANDWICH STAR decanter, goblet, spoonholder.
2. HARP spoonholder, handled lamp, footed salt.
3. RAY plate (six inch), sugar bowl, celery vase.
4. ENGLISH HOBNAIL and THUMBPRINT bowl, fruit dish, sauce dish.

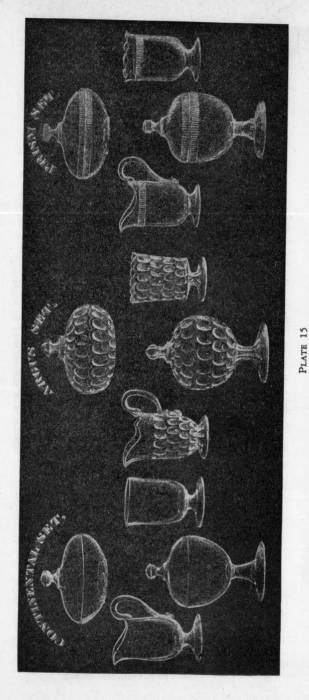

PLATE 15

Page from Bakewell, Pears & Co. catalogue, showing "sets" of Continental, Argus (now known as Thumbprint) and Prism (now known as Prism and Flute).

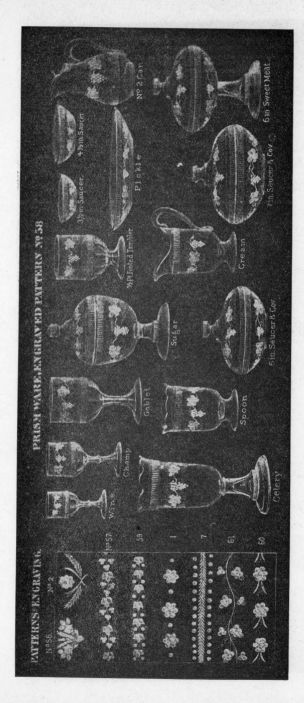

PLATE 16

Page from Bakewell, Pears & Co. catalogue, showing Prism pattern, engraved, together with patterns used for engraving.

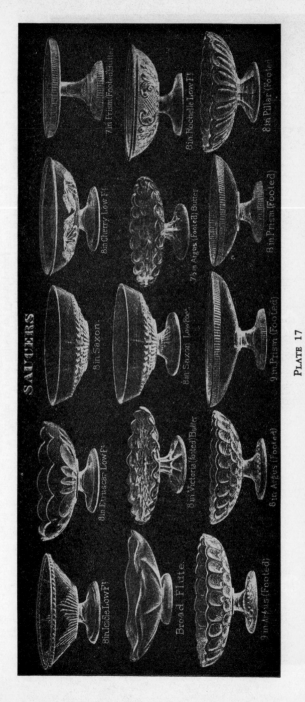

SAUCERS

7 in. Prism (Footed) Butter
8 in. Rochelle Low Ft
8 in. Pillar (Footed)

8 in. Cherry Low Ft
7½ in. Argus (Footed) Butter
8 in. Prism (Footed)

8 in. Saxon.
8 in. Saxon Low Foot
9 in. Prism (Footed)

8 in. Etrusca Low Ft
8 in. Victoria (footed) Butter
8 in. Argus (footed)

8 in. Icicle Low Ft
Broad Flute.
9 in. Argus (Footed)

PLATE 17

Page from Bakewell, Pears & Co. catalogue, showing their "saucers" and footed butter dishes.

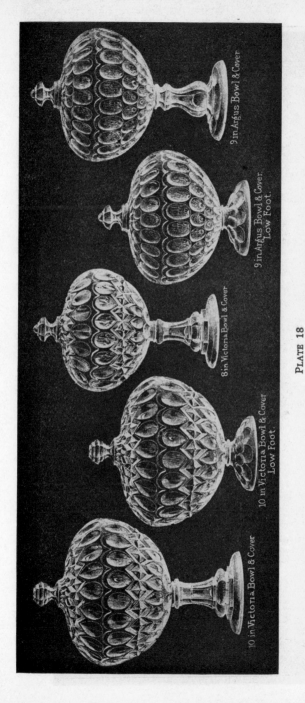

10 in Victoria Bowl & Cover.

10 in Victoria Bowl & Cover.
Low Foot.

8 in Victoria Bowl & Cover.

9 in Argus Bowl & Cover.
Low Foot.

9 in Argus Bowl & Cover.

PLATE 18

Group of covered compotes in the Victoria and Argus patterns, of the Bakewell, Pears & Co.
(Argus is now known as Thumbprint).

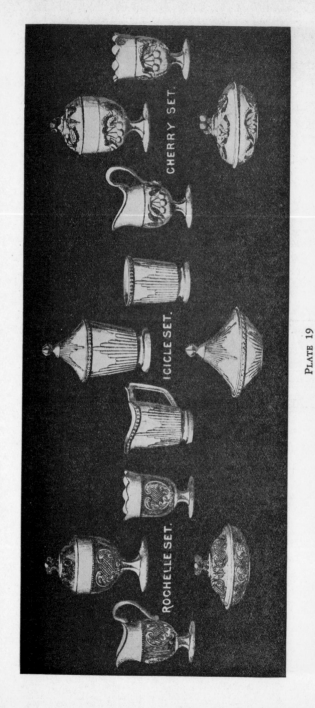

PLATE 19

"Sets" showing Rochelle, Icicle and Cherry patterns, taken directly from the old trade catalogue of Bakewell, Pears & Co., Pittsburgh, Pa. (Rochelle is now known as Princess Feather).

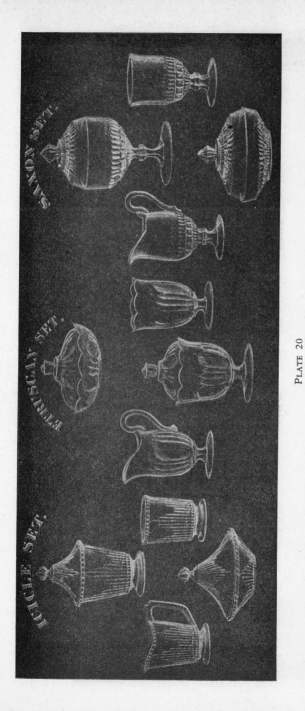

PLATE 20

"Sets," showing Icicle, Etruscan and Saxon patterns, taken directly from the old trade catalogue of Bakewell, Pears & Co., Pittsburgh, Pa.

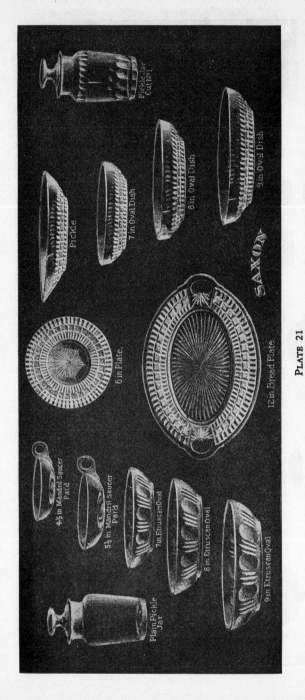

Pickle Jar Cut No 1

Pickle

7 in Oval Dish

8 in Oval Dish

9 in Oval Dish

SAXON

6 in Plate.

12 in Bread Plate

4½ in Mandarı Saucer Pat'd

5½ in Mandarı Saucer Pat'd

7 in Etruscan Oval

8 in Etruscan Oval

9 in Etruscan Oval

Plain Pickle Jar

PLATE 21

Page taken from Bakewell, Pears & Co., trade catalogue, illustrating Saxon pattern.

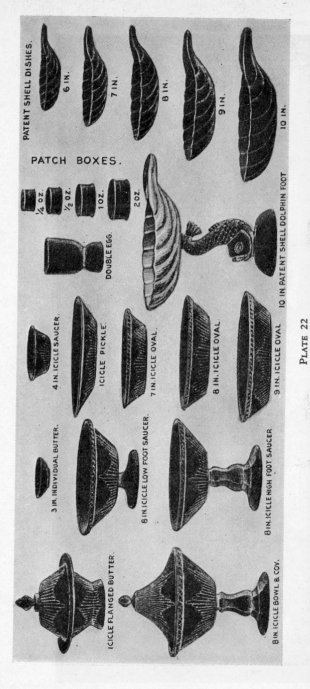

PATENT SHELL DISHES.

6 IN.
7 IN.
8 IN.
9 IN.
10 IN.

PATCH BOXES.

¼ OZ.
½ OZ.
1 OZ.
2 OZ.

DOUBLE EGG.

10 IN. PATENT SHELL DOLPHIN FOOT

4 IN. ICICLE SAUCER.

ICICLE PICKLE.

7 IN. ICICLE OVAL.

8 IN. ICICLE OVAL.

9 IN. ICICLE OVAL.

3 IN. INDIVIDUAL BUTTER.

8 IN. ICICLE LOW FOOT SAUCER.

8 IN. ICICLE HIGH FOOT SAUCER.

ICICLE FLANGED BUTTER.

8 IN. ICICLE BOWL & COV.

PLATE 22

Group of Icicle pattern and Dolphin dish, as taken from the old trade catalogue of Bakewell, Pears & Co., of Pittsburgh, Pa.

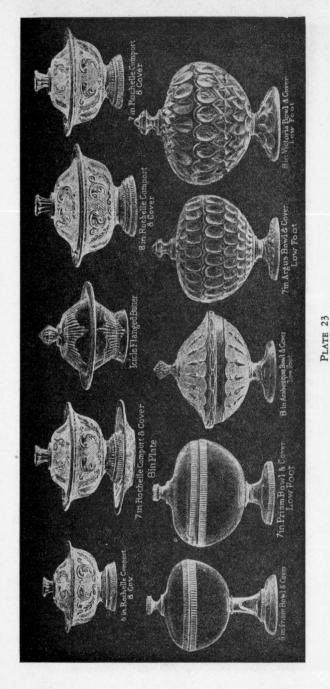

PLATE 23

Group of covered dishes, taken from old trade catalogue of Bakewell, Pears & Co., Pittsburgh, Pa.

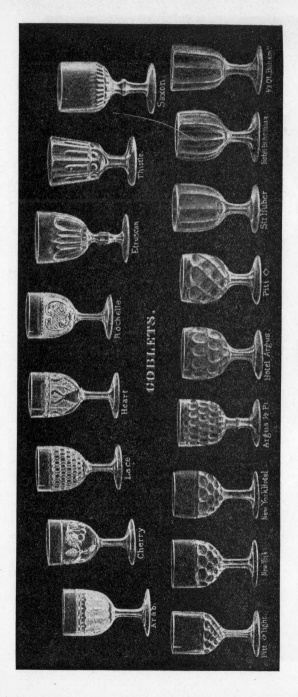

GOBLETS.

Arab.   Cherry   Lace   Heart   Rochelle   Etruscan   Thistle   Saxon

Pitt ◇ light.   New York   New York flutel   Argus ½ Pt.   Hotel Argus   Pitt ◇   St. Huber   Hotel Bohemian   ½ Qt. Bohem.

PLATE 24

Group of goblets, in patterns made by Bakewell, Pears & Co.

PLATE 25
Diamond Thumbprint
Popcorn Pattern

PLATE 26—GOBLETS

Waffle and Thumbprint	Cube
Lincoln Drape	Lincoln Drape with Tassel

PLATE 27—GOBLETS

Bull's Eye with Diamond Points   Ribbed Grape
Prism   Fine Rib

PLATE 28—GOBLETS

Stippled Medallion   Arched Leaf
Pillar   Variation of the "Pillar"

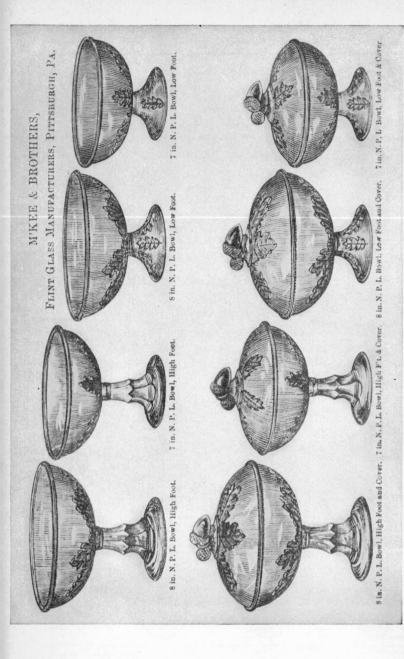

M'KEE & BROTHERS,
FLINT GLASS MANUFACTURERS, PITTSBURGH, PA.

7 in. N. P. L. Bowl, Low Foot.

8 in. N. P. L. Bowl, Low Foot.

7 in. N. P. L. Bowl, High Foot.

8 in. N. P. L. Bowl, High Foot.

7 in. N. P. L. Bowl, Low Foot & Cover.

8 in. N. P. L. Bowl, Low Foot and Cover.

7 in. N. P. L. Bowl, High F't. & Cover.

8 in. N. P. L. Bowl, High Foot and Cover.

PLATE 29

Groups showing the "N. P. L." pattern of M'Kee & Brothers, as shown in their trade catalogue.

M'KEE & BROTHERS, FLINT GLASS MANUFACTURERS, PITTSBURGH, PA.

½ gall. N. P. L. Pitcher.

N. P. L. Salt.

6 in. N. P. L. Nappie & Cover.

4 in. N. P. L. Nappie.

7 in. N. P. L. Dish.

N. P. L. Egg.

N. P. L. Wine.

8 in. N. P. L. Dish.

N. P. L. Spoon.

N. P. L. Champagne.

N. P. L. Goblet.

9 in. N. P. L. Dish.

N. P. L. Cream.

N. P. L. Sugar.

6 in. N. P. L. Sweetmeat & Cover.

PLATE 29A

Group showing the "N. P. L." pattern of M'Kee & Brothers, as shown in their trade catalogue.
This pattern is now known as Pressed Leaf.

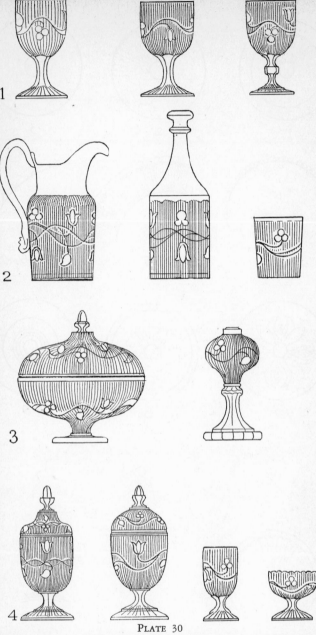

PLATE 30

1. BELLFLOWER goblet with coarse rib; barrel shaped goblet with
   fine rib; barrel goblet, fine rib, knob stem.
2. BELLFLOWER water pitcher with double vine; decanter with
   double vine and bar lip, tumbler.
3. BELLFLOWER covered compote on low foot, lamp.
4. BELLFLOWER sugar bowl with double vine; sugar bowl with
   single vine, egg cup, salt.

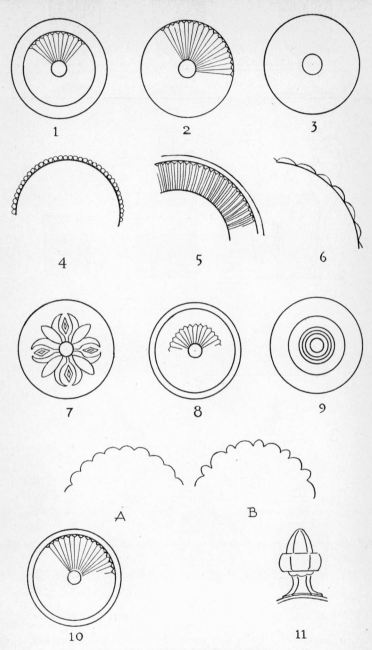

PLATE 31—BELLFLOWER DETAILS

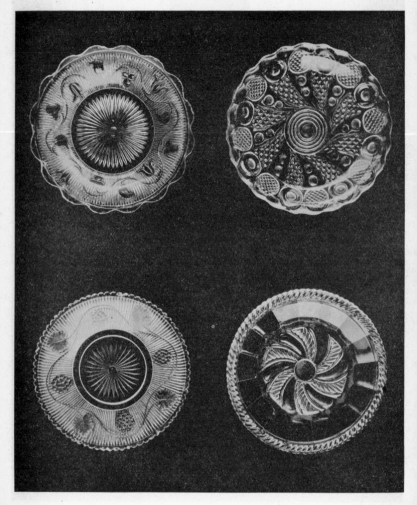

PLATE 32—SIX INCH PLATES

| Bellflower | Horn of Plenty |
| Ribbed Grape | Cable |

PLATE 33—GOBLETS

Ivy   Bellflower
Ribbed Palm   Inverted Fern

PLATE 34

1. BELLFLOWER castor set in pewter standard, celery vase, footed tumbler.
2. RIBBED VARIANTS of BELLFLOWER ERA.
3. Candlesticks in EXCELSIOR pattern. One of the earliest pressed glass designs to match table ware.

RIBBED GRAPE COMPOTE   OPAL BELLFLOWER EGG CUPS

PLATE 35

PLATE 36

1. RIBBED GRAPE creamer, sugar bowl, spoonholder.
2. FINE RIB goblet, covered compote on low foot, footed salt, cordial.
3. INVERTED FERN sugar bowl, butter dish, egg cup, sauce dish.
4. CABLE goblet, open compote, footed salt, egg cup.

PLATE 37—SIX INCH PLATES

Tulip   Waffle
Ribbed Palm   Rayed, with Loop border

M'KEE & BROTHERS,

FLINT GLASS MANUFACTURERS, PITTSBURGH, PA.

6 in. Sprig Nappy and Cover.

6 in. Sprig Sweetmeat and Cover.

6 in. Sprig Nappy

4 in. Sprig Nappy.

7 in. Sprig Bowl, Low Foot.

6 in. Sprig Plate.

8 in. Sprig Bowl, High Foot.

8 in. Sprig Bowl, Low Foot.

½ gall. Sprig Pitcher.

PLATE 38

Group of Ribbed Palm, originally termed "Sprig," as shown by M'Kee & Brothers of Pittsburgh, Pa., in the late Sixties.

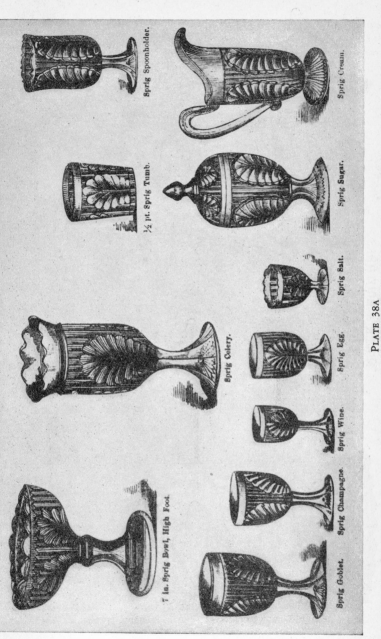

McKEE & BROTHERS, FLINT GLASS MANUFACTURERS, PITTSBURGH, PA.

Sprig Spoonholder.

Sprig Cream.

½ pt. Sprig Tumb.

Sprig Sugar.

Sprig Salt.

Sprig Celery.

Sprig Egg.

Sprig Wine.

7 in. Sprig Bowl, High Foot.

Sprig Champagne.

Sprig Goblet.

PLATE 38A

Group of Ribbed Palm, originally termed "Sprig," as shown by McKee & Brothers of Pittsburgh, Pa., in the late Sixties.

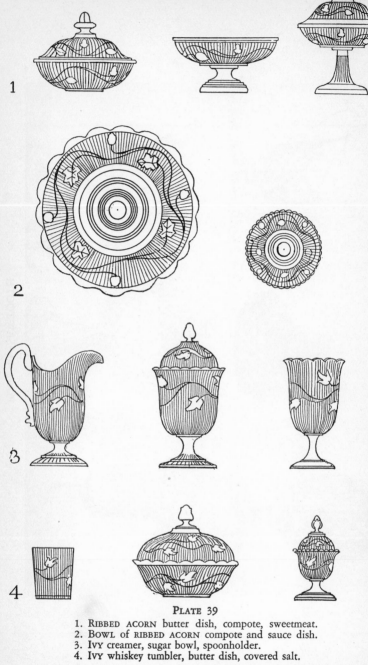

PLATE 39

1. RIBBED ACORN butter dish, compote, sweetmeat.
2. BOWL of RIBBED ACORN compote and sauce dish.
3. IVY creamer, sugar bowl, spoonholder.
4. IVY whiskey tumbler, butter dish, covered salt.

PLATE 40—SAWTOOTH

Sugar bowl   Wine glass   Butter dish   Pomade jar   Creamer
Pair of celery vases   Pair of candlesticks   Compote on high foot

PLATE 41—SAWTOOTH OF LATER PERIOD

Pair of covered dishes with lion handles and knobs   Open compote in center

Sugar bowl   Cake plate on standard   Creamer

PLATE 42—GOBLETS

New England Pineapple   Tulip

Sawtooth   Diamond Point

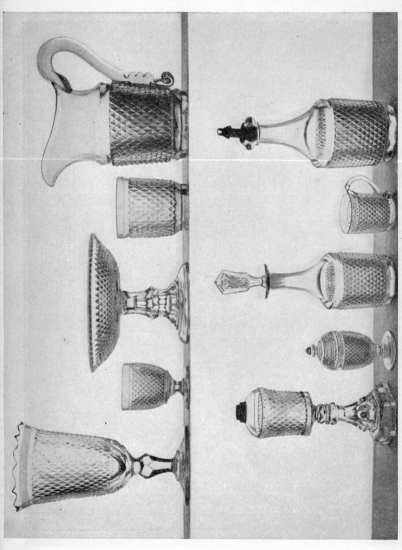

PLATE 43—GROUP OF DIAMOND POINT

Celery vase   Egg cup   Open compote   Tumbler   Water pitcher

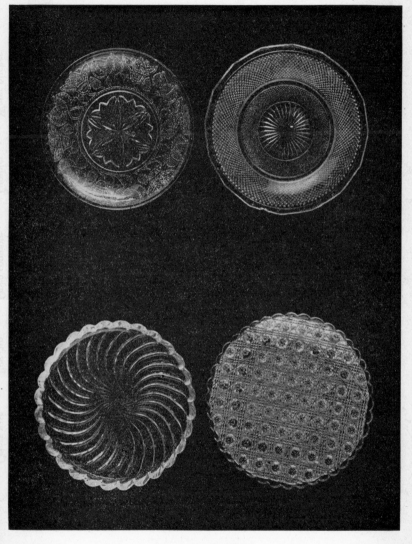

PLATE 44—PLATES

Beaded Tulip   Diamond Point
Pinwheel   Daisy

PLATE 45—PLATES

Diamond Point, star and circle center   Diamond Point, star center
Willow Oak   Single Tulip

PLATE 46

1. WAFFLE celery vase, water tumbler, butter dish, egg cup.
2. LINCOLN DRAPE compote, syrup pitcher, spoonholder, butter dish.
3. LINCOLN DRAPE compote, bowl of sauce dish, footed salt, egg cup.
4. LINCOLN DRAPE with TASSEL goblet, compote, spoonholder.

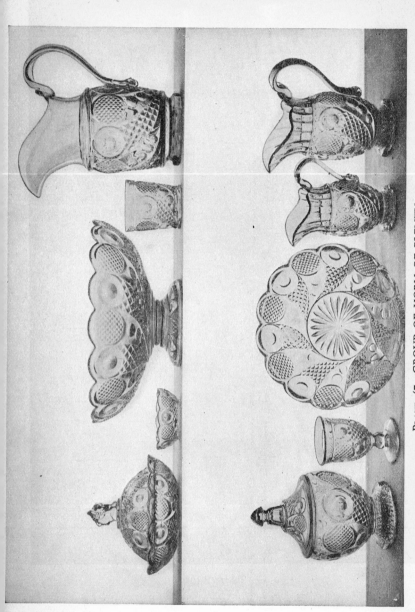

PLATE 47—GROUP OF HORN OF PLENTY

Rare butter dish with knob in form of Washington's head, oval salt, compote, tumbler, water pitcher

PLATE 48—GOBLETS

Bull's Eye with Fleur de Lys   Bull's Eye

Comet   Horn of Plenty

PLATE 49

1. BULL'S EYE goblet with knob stem; goblet, simple stem; cordial; egg cup; salt.
2. BULL'S EYE pickle dish, sugar bowl, tumbler.
3. COMET goblet, water pitcher, whiskey tumbler.
4. BULL'S EYE with DIAMOND POINT celery vase, cruet, egg cup, bowl of sauce dish.

PLATE 50

1. TULIP VARIANTS (later period) sugar bowl, goblet, cordial, celery variant without sawtooth at base of petals.
2. BULL'S EYE VARIANT goblet, footed tumbler, water tumbler, castor bottle.
3. JACOB'S LADDER creamer, jam jar, plate, cordial.
4. WHEAT and BARLEY handled cup, celery vase, water pitcher, footed sauce dish.

PLATE 51—BULL'S EYE WITH FLEUR DE LYS

Goblet   Sugar bowl

W, no. inches   Lamp

PLATE 52—SIX INCH PLATES

Diamond Quilted with Bull's Eye border   New England Pineapple

Tree of Life   **Garfield**

PLATE 53

1. TULIP butter dish, creamer, pomade jar.
2. TULIP celery vase, quart decanter with original patent stopper (Tulip stopper in insert), cordial, footed salt.
3. NEW ENGLAND PINEAPPLE open compote on high foot, creamer, sugar bowl.
4. NEW ENGLAND PINEAPPLE tumbler, sauce dish, egg cup.

PLATE 54—TULIP

Pair of large cruets, pair of smaller cruets and butter dish.

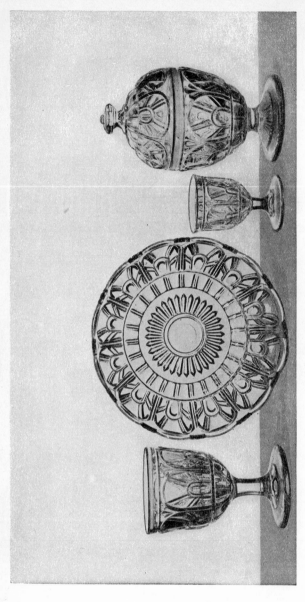

PLATE 55—GOTHIC

Goblet   Bowl   Egg cup   Sugar bowl

PLATE 56—HAMILTON

Egg cup   Tumbler   Creamer   Butter dish   Spoonholder
Sugar bowl   Compote   Water pitcher   Goblet

PLATE 57—GOBLETS

Dew with Raindrop   Beaded Dewdrop

Hamilton with Leaf   Jacob's Ladder

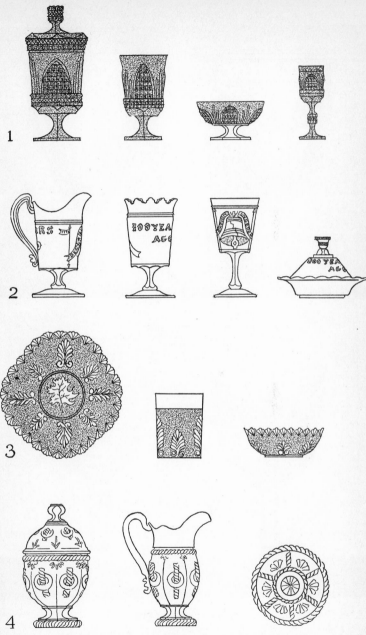

PLATE 58

1. CATHEDRAL sugar bowl, spoonholder, footed sauce dish, cordial.
2. LIBERTY BELL creamer, spoonholder, goblet, butter dish.
3. ANTHEMION plate with rolled edges, tumbler, sauce dish.
4. CABLE with RING sugar bowl, creamer, bowl of sauce dish.

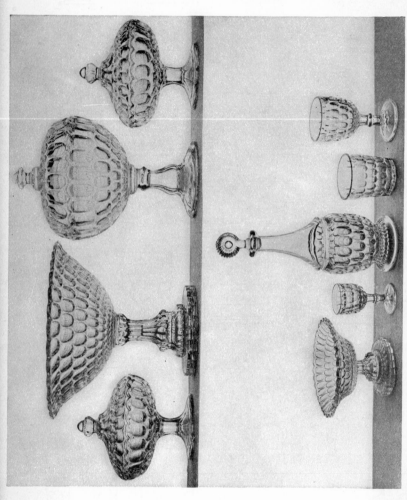

PLATE 59—THUMBPRINT

Pair of covered compotes   Large open compote   Covered compote

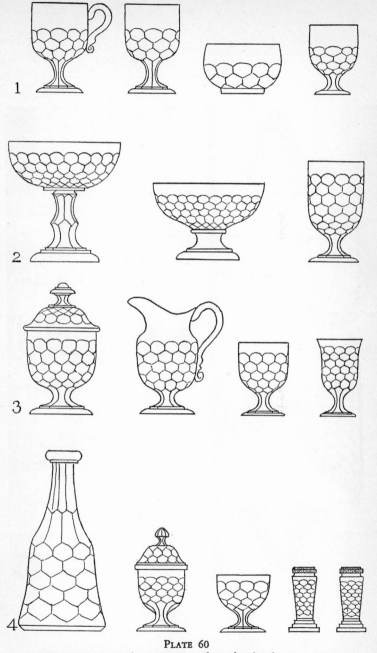

PLATE 60

1. HONEYCOMB custard cup, egg cup, finger bowl, salt.
2. HONEYCOMB compote on high foot, compote on low foot, celery vase.
3. HONEYCOMB sugar bowl, creamer, two styles of egg cups.
4. HONEYCOMB decanter, covered salt, open salt, shakers.

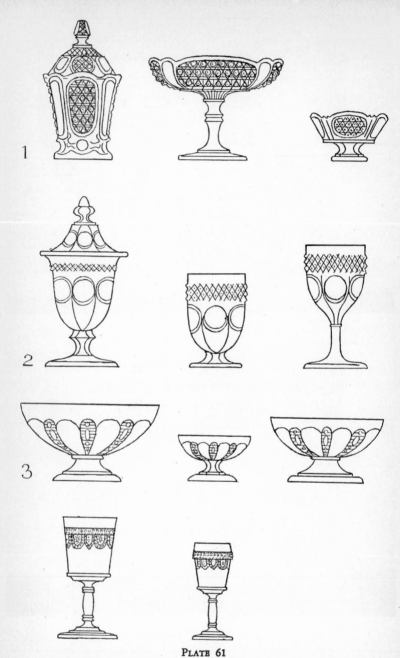

PLATE 61

1. FINE CUT and PANEL sugar bowl, compote, footed sauce dish.
2. BAND sugar bowl, footed tumbler, goblet.
3. PHILADELPHIA compote on low foot, footed sauce, smaller compote.
4. BEADED BAND goblet, cordial.

PLATE 62—GOBLETS

Magnet and Grape
Banded Buckle

Oval Panel
Buckle

PLATE 63

1. BEADED GRAPE celery vase, tumbler, butter dish, creamer.
2. MAGNET and GRAPE (frosted leaf) goblet, tumbler, creamer, salt.
3. GRAPE and FESTOON goblet (stippled leaf), butter dish, creamer, goblet (clear leaf).
4. STIPPLED GRAPE and FESTOON celery vase, creamer, goblets (clear and stippled leaf).

PLATE 64

1. PANELLED GRAPE celery vase, spoonholder, water pitcher.
2. PANELLED GRAPE sugar bowl, creamer, goblet.
3. ARCHED GRAPE goblet, spoonholder, creamer, butter dish.
4. GRAPE BAND goblet, creamer, spoonholder, cordial.

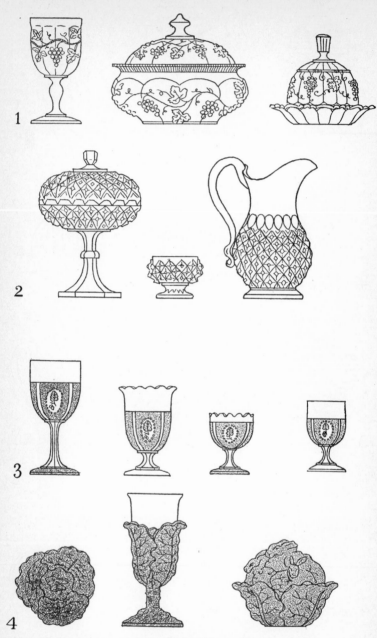

PLATE 65

1. LATE PANELLED GRAPE goblet, covered bowl, butter dish.
2. FLATTENED SAWTOOTH compote, footed salt, water pitcher.
3. BEADED ACORN goblet, spoonholder, footed salt, egg cup.
4. CABBAGE LEAF bowl of sauce dish, celery vase, butter dish.

PLATE 66

1. BALTIMORE PEAR sugar bowl, water pitcher, spoonholder.
2. CHERRY goblet, sugar bowl, bowl of sauce dish.
3. BEADED GRAPE MEDALLION (banded) covered compote, pickle dish, creamer.
4. BEADED GRAPE MEDALLION goblets and their different bases.

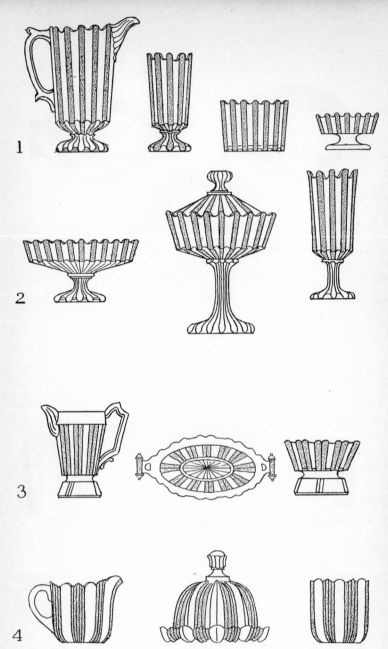

PLATE 67

1. RIBBON water pitcher, spoonholder, bowl, footed sauce dish.
2. RIBBON compote on low foot, compote on high standard, celery vase.
3. DOUBLE RIBBON creamer, pickle dish, footed sauce dish.
4. FLUTED RIBBON creamer, butter dish, spoonholder.

PLATE 68

Pair of relish dishes with frosted centers, plate in Frosted Stork Dolphin
dish with bowl in Ribbon pattern, Ribbon goblets.

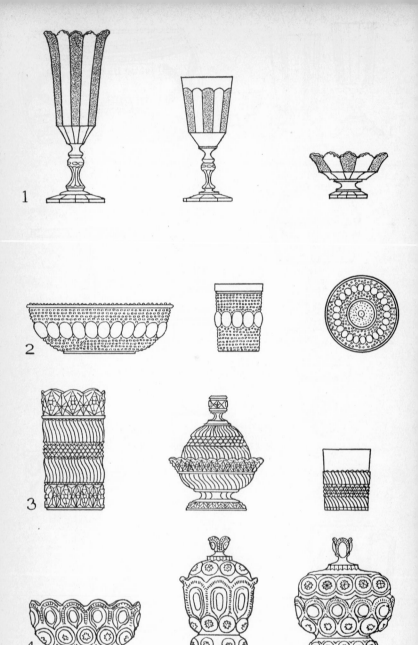

PLATE 69

1. FROSTED RIBBON celery vase, goblet, footed sauce dish.
2. DEW and RAINDROP berry bowl, tumbler, bowl of sauce dish.
3. SWIRL celery vase, butter dish, tumbler.
4. MOON and STAR berry bowl, sugar bowl, covered dish.

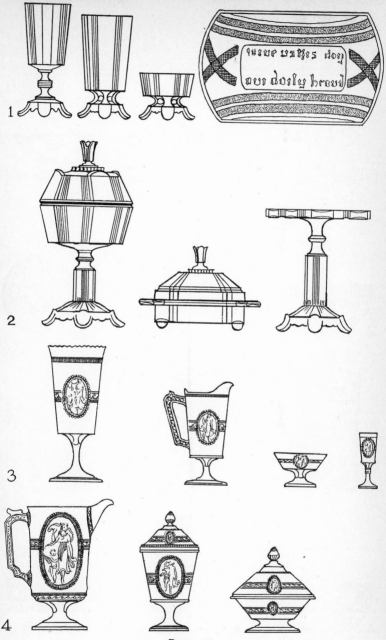

PLATE 70

1. CLEAR RIBBON goblet, spoonholder, sauce dish, bread tray.
2. CLEAR RIBBON compote, butter dish, cake plate on standard.
3. CUPID and VENUS celery vase, creamer, footed sauce dish, cordial.
4. CUPID and VENUS water pitcher, sugar bowl, butter dish.

PLATE 71—GOBLETS

Hobnail with Fan top   Flattened Hobnail
Dewdrop   Popcorn

PLATE 72—GOBLETS

"101"   Panelled Dewdrop
Printed Hobnail   Late Buckle

PLATE 73—LARGE PLATES

Rose in Snow   Dewdrop with Star
Dewdrop with Sheaf of Wheat   Arched Leaf

PLATE 74—SEVEN INCH PLATES

Stippled Forget-me-not   Snakeskin with Dot, three sizes
Hobnail   "101"

PLATE 75

1. PSYCHE and CUPID sugar bowl, goblet, celery vase.
2. CLEMATIS goblet, spoonholder, bowl of sauce dish.
3. JEWEL with DEWDROP pitcher, sauce dish, cordial.
4. PANELLED DEWDROP celery vase, lemonade, goblet.

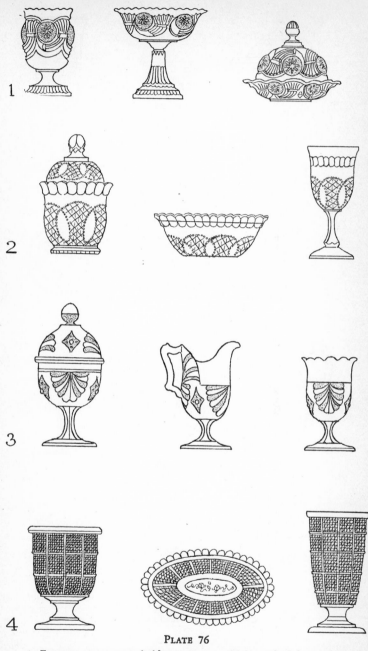

PLATE 76

1. FROSTED CIRCLE spoonholder, compote on high standard, butter dish.
2. BEADED LOOP sugar bowl, bowl (cover missing), goblet.
3. FAN with DIAMOND sugar bowl, creamer, spoonholder.
4. PLAID sugar bowl (cover missing), pickle dish, celery vase.

PLATE 77

1. BEADED OVAL and SCROLL goblet, creamer, bowl of sauce dish.
2. PANELLED FLOWER STIPPLED spoonholder, oval dish, sugar bowl.
3. SWAN creamer, oval covered dish, goblet.
4. FORGET-ME-NOT and SCROLL creamer, sugar bowl, spoonholder.

PLATE 78

1. LATTICE sugar bowl, butter dish, goblet.
2. SPRIG goblet, open compote, sauce dish.
3. TEARDROP and TASSEL compote, water pitcher, sauce dish.
4. DIAMOND SUNBURST water pitcher, goblet, bowl of sauce dish.

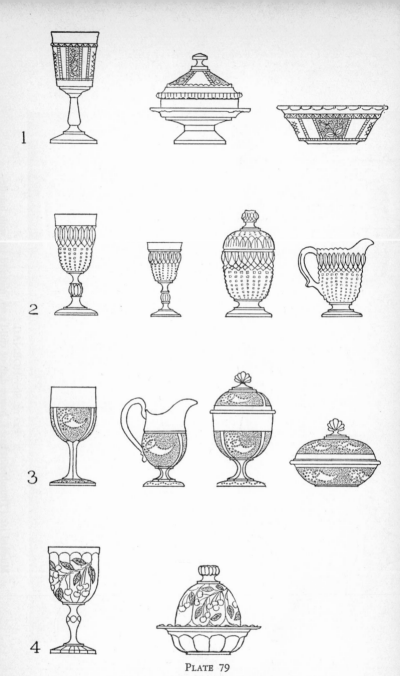

PLATE 79

1. PANELLED FORGET-ME-NOT goblet, butter dish, bowl (cover missing).
2. LOOP with DEWDROPS goblet, cordial, sugar bowl, creamer.
3. POWDER and SHOT goblet, creamer, sugar bowl, butter dish.
4. PANELLED CHERRY goblet, butter dish.

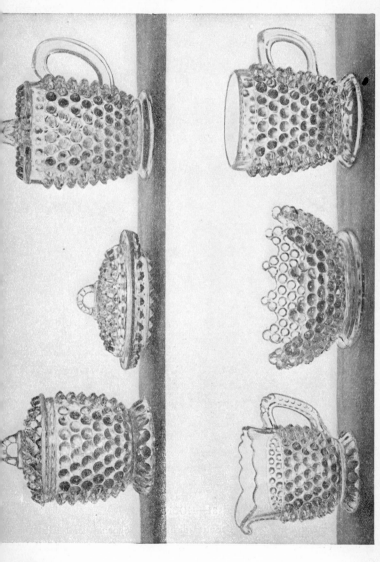

PLATE 80—HOBNAIL

Mustard jar (Thumbprint base), butter dish of child's set, mustard jar with handle
Creamer (Thumbprint base), sauce dish, handled mug (Thumbprint base).

PLATE 81—HOBNAIL

Creamer	Butter dish	Spoonholder (Ball feet)
Finger bowl (Thumbprint base)	Goblet	Open sugar (Ball feet)

PLATE 82—HOBNAIL

Salt and pepper shakers   Butter dish of child's set   Cup
Sugar bowl of child's set   Tumbler   Cordial   Cup showing ornamented band

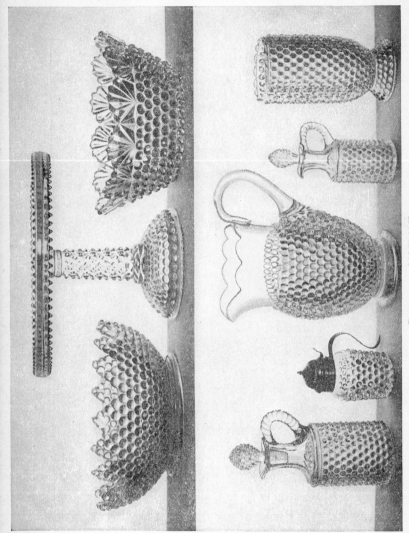

PLATE 83—HOBNAIL

Bowl on bowl with pissing high edge · · · C la pig on stan l · · · Bowl on bowl with fan ice

1

2

3

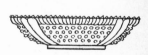

4

PLATE 84

1. OPAL HOBNAIL (frilled top) celery vase, creamer, tumbler.
2. OPAL HOBNAIL (three feet) celery vase, creamer, tumbler.
3. OPAL HOBNAIL (four feet) sugar bowl, creamer, butter dish.
4. PANELLED HOBNAIL compote, berry bowl.

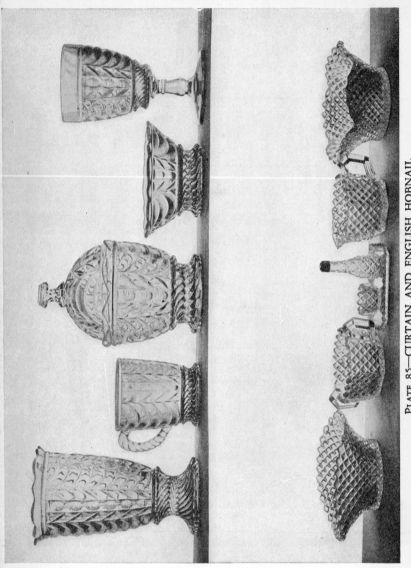

PLATE 85—CURTAIN AND ENGLISH HOBNAIL

Cup in relay ware   Handled mug   Sugar bowl   Sauce dish   Goblet

PLATE 86—GOBLETS

Panelled Diamond Point   English Hobnail, Panelled
Forget-Me-Not in Scroll   Rose Sprig

PLATE 87—LARGE PLATES

English Hobnail and Thumbprint   Daisy and Button

Dewdrop in Points, vine border

PLATE 88—HOBNAIL

Tray for water set   Plate in Panelled Hobnail

Saucers for cups illustrated on Plate 82

PLATE 89

1. WESTWARD-HO compote, sugar bowl, creamer, marmalade jar.
2. WESTWARD-HO butter dish, celery vase, footed sauce dish.
3. THREE-FACE compote, salt shaker, sugar bowl, compote.
4. BABY-FACE sugar bowl, spoonholder, goblet.

PLATE 90—GROUP OF WESTWARD-HO

PLATE 91—GOBLETS

Lion   Three-Face
Polar Bear   Westward-Ho

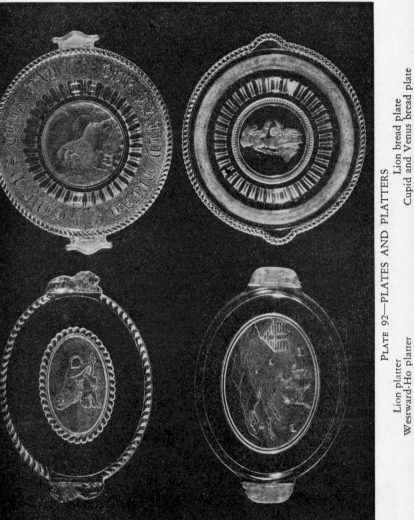

PLATE 92—PLATES AND PLATTERS

Lion platter   Lion bread plate
Westward-Ho platter   Cupid and Venus bread plate

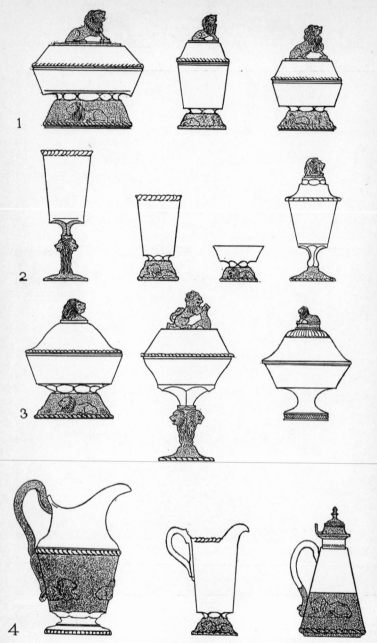

PLATE 93

1. LION oblong covered dish, sugar bowl, butter dish.
2. LION celery vase, spoonholder, footed sauce, sugar bowl.
3. LION covered dish, compote on high standard, compote on low foot.
4. LION water pitcher, creamer, syrup pitcher.

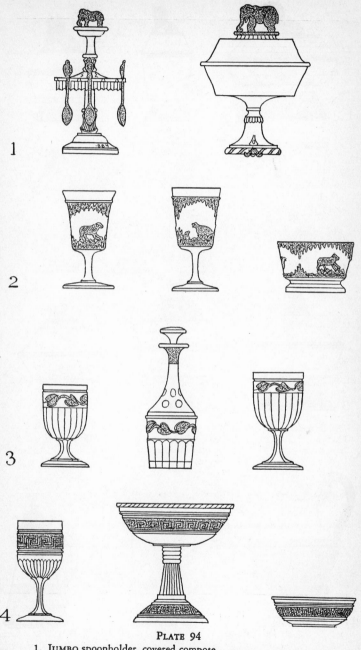

PLATE 94

1. JUMBO spoonholder, covered compote.
2. POLAR BEAR clear goblet, goblet frosted and clear, bowl.
3. FROSTED LEAF spoonholder, decanter, goblet.
4. ROMAN KEY goblet, open compote on high standard, sauce dish.

PLATE 95—CELERY VASES

Palmette   Panelled Daisy
Roman Key   Leaf and Dart

PLATE 96—GOBLETS

Three Panel
Teasel

Frosted Circle
Prism with Diamond Points

PLATE 97—CLASSIC—SHELL AND TASSEL

Classic spoonholder   Butter dish   Sugar bowl (cover missing)   Creamer

PLATE 98—GOBLETS

| Garfield Drape | Cardinal Bird |
| Star Rosetted | Classic |

PLATE 99—COVERED DISHES

Pair of compotes with frosted eagle knobs
Compote with knob in form of large dog, frosted

Pair of oval dishes with knobs in form of pheasants, frosted
Frosted Stork sugar bowl

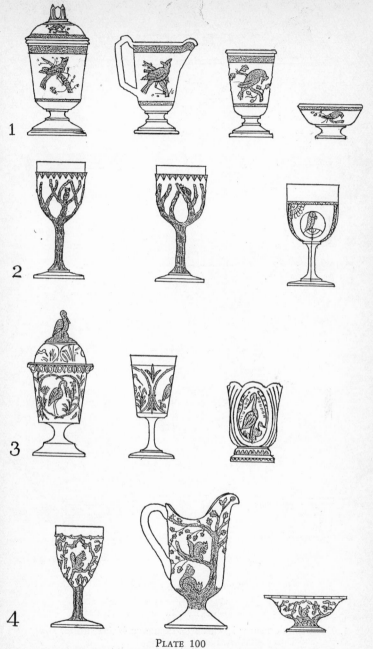

PLATE 100

1. CARDINAL BIRD sugar bowl, creamer, spoonholder, footed sauce dish.
2. OWL and POSSUM goblet, showing both sides of bowl, PARROT goblet.
3. FROSTED STORK sugar bowl, goblet, spoonholder.
4. SQUIRREL goblet, water pitcher, footed sauce dish.

PLATE 101

1. DEER and DOG sugar bowl, Dog compote on high standard, Deer and Dog covered compote.
2. DOUBLE LOOP creamer, spoonholder, butter dish.
3. STIPPLED DAISY creamer, spoonholder, oblong dish.
4. BLOCK with THUMBPRINT goblet, footed tumbler goblet in later copy of same pattern.

PLATE 102

1. HONEYCOMB with STAR butter dish, sugar bowl, creamer, spoon-holder.
2. MEDALLION water pitcher, butter dish, goblet.
3. BANDED BUCKLE sugar bowl, egg cup, spoonholder.
4. BUCKLE sugar bowl, creamer, egg cup, bowl of sauce dish.

PLATE 103—GOBLETS

Moon and Star   Gooseberry

Ivy in Snow   Diamond Band

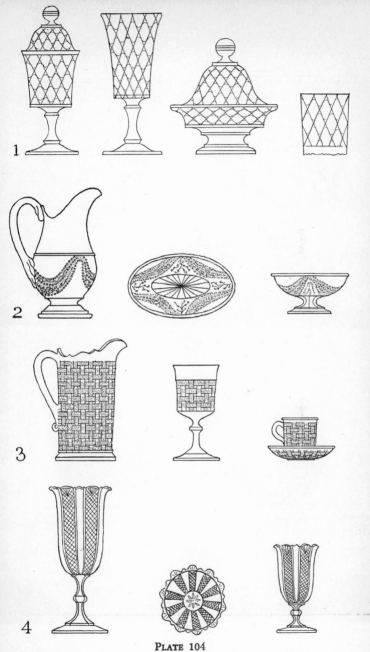

PLATE 104

1. DIAMOND QUILTED sugar bowl, celery vase, butter dish, tumbler.
2. GARFIELD DRAPE water pitcher, pickle dish, footed sauce dish.
3. BASKET WEAVE water pitcher, goblet, cup and saucer.
4. PANELLED DIAMOND POINT celery vase, bowl of sauce dish, spoonholder.

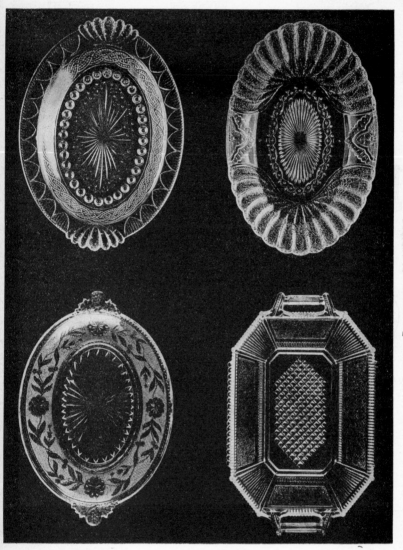

PLATE 105—PLATTERS

Dahlia

Chain and Shield

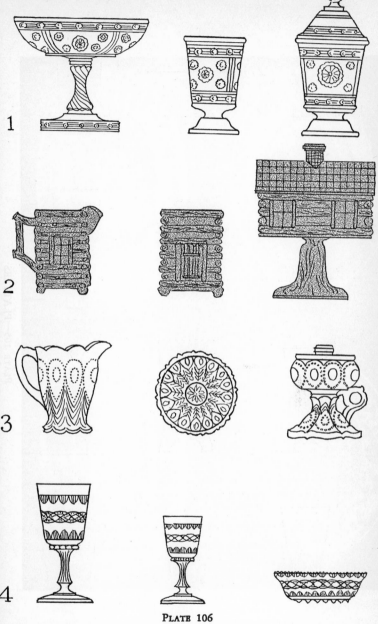

PLATE 106

1. ROSETTE compote, spoonholder, sugar bowl.
2. LOG CABIN creamer, spoonholder, compote.
3. PEACOCK FEATHER (late) creamer, bowl of sauce dish, handled lamp.
4. SHIELD and CHAIN goblet, cordial, sauce dish.

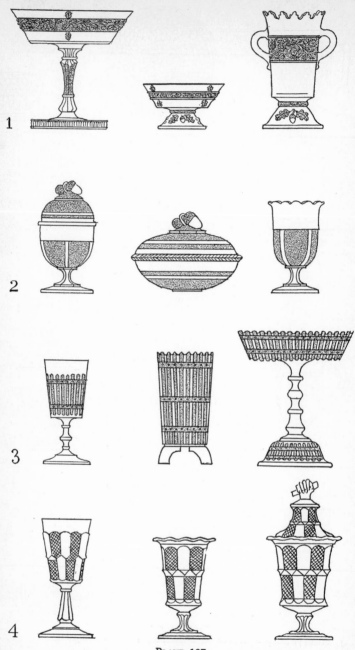

PLATE 107

1. FLOWER BAND compote, footed sauce dish, celery vase.
2. STIPPLED BAND sugar bowl, butter dish, spoonholder.
3. PICKET goblet, celery vase, open compote on high standard.
4. HAND goblet, spoonholder, sugar bowl.

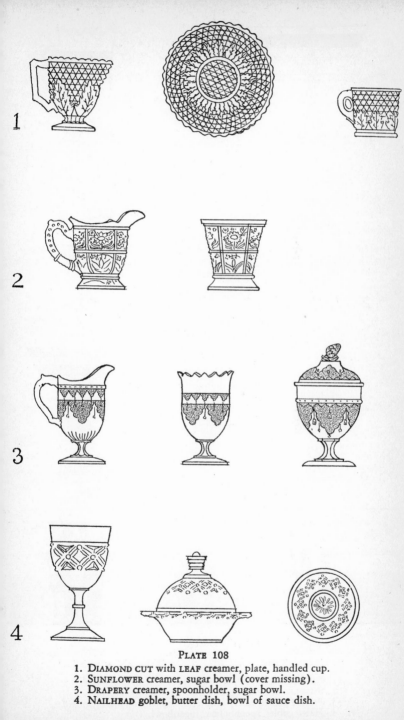

PLATE 108

1. DIAMOND CUT with LEAF creamer, plate, handled cup.
2. SUNFLOWER creamer, sugar bowl (cover missing).
3. DRAPERY creamer, spoonholder, sugar bowl.
4. NAILHEAD goblet, butter dish, bowl of sauce dish.

PLATE 109—GOBLETS

Roman Rosette   Diamond Cut with Leaf
Princess Feather   Flower Band

PLATE 110
Tray in "Currier and Ives" pattern
Railroad Train platter

PLATE 111—GOBLETS

Pleat and Panel   Canadian
Cupid and Venus   Egyptian

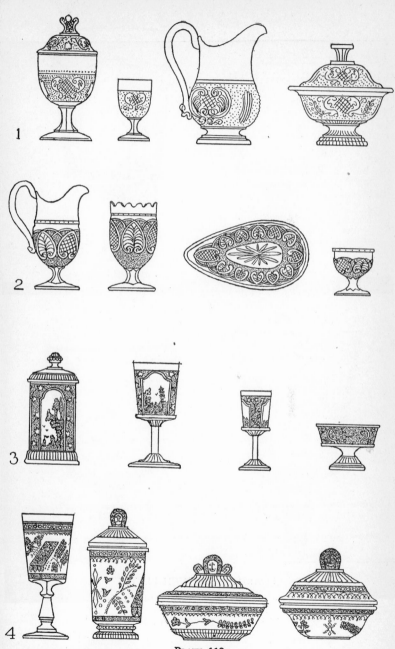

PLATE 112

1. PRINCESS FEATHER sugar bowl, egg cup, water pitcher, covered bowl.
2. PALMETTE creamer, spoonholder, pickle dish, footed salt.
3. CANADIAN jam jar, goblet, cordial, footed sauce dish.
4. HORSESHOE or GOOD LUCK goblet, jam jar, covered bowl, butter dish.

PLATE 113—SIX INCH PLATES

Grape   Barley
Liberty Bell   Canadian

PLATE 114—LARGE PLATES

Wheat and Barley   Primrose
Panelled Thistle   Cap Cod

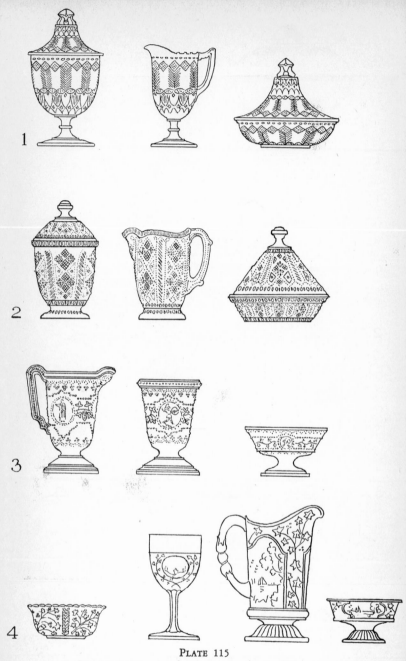

PLATE 115

1. HERRINGBONE sugar bowl, creamer, butter dish.
2. JACOB'S COAT sugar bowl, creamer, butter dish.
3. MINERVA creamer, spoonholder, footed sauce.
4. CAPE COD sauce dish, goblet, water pitcher, footed sauce.

PLATE 116

1. HOLLY covered compote, goblet, egg cup.
2. CORD and TASSEL wine, celery vase, water pitcher.
3. BARLEY celery vase, jam jar, footed sauce, goblet.
4. BEADED TULIP butter dish, sugar bowl, footed sauce, goblet.

PLATE 117—PLATTERS AND GOBLETS

Prescott and Stark, "The Heroes of Bunker Hill"

Liberty Bell

PLATE 118—BREAD PLATES

Scroll with Flowers   Grape

Egyptian   Centennial, with eagle

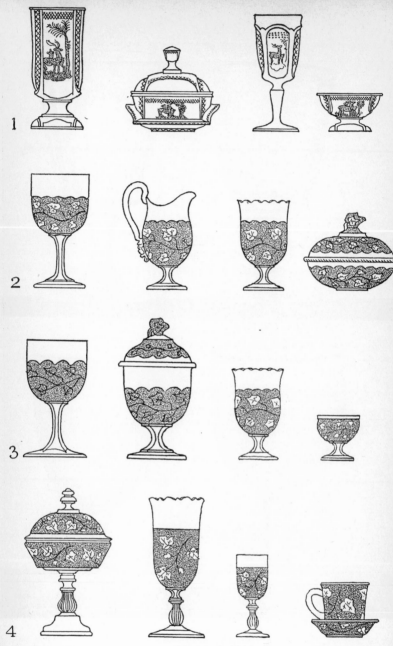

PLATE 119

1. DEER and PINE TREE celery vase, butter dish, goblet, footed sauce dish.
2. BUDDED IVY goblet, creamer, spoonholder, butter dish.
3. STIPPLED IVY goblet, sugar bowl, spoonholder, footed salt.
4. IVY in SNOW covered compote, celery vase, cordial, cup and saucer.

PLATE 120—GOBLETS

Rose in Snow   Fishscale

Palmette   Windflower

PLATE 121—GOBLETS

Arabesque   Minerva
Herringbone   Drapery

PLATE 122

1. ROSE in SNOW (square) creamer, sugar bowl, butter dish.
2. ROSE in SNOW (round) sugar bowl, creamer, handled cup,
   covered compote on high standard.
3. OPEN ROSE sugar bowl, creamer, egg cup.
4. CABBAGE ROSE goblet, covered compote, cordial.

PLATE 123—GOBLETS

Open Rose
Lily of the Valley

Wildflower
Bleeding Heart

PLATE 124—SIX INCH PLATES

Rose Sprig, Beaded Acorn, Stippled Cherry, Loop and Dart with
Diamond Ornaments

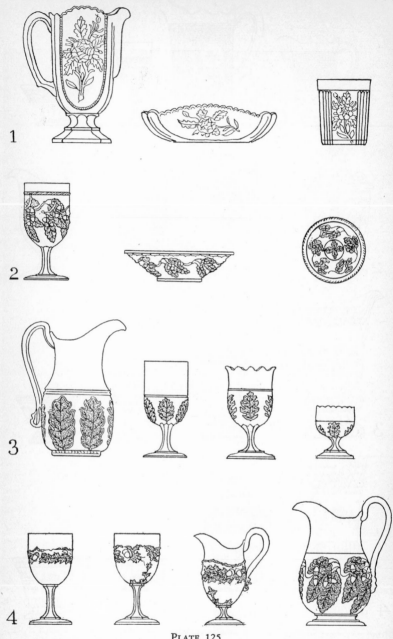

PLATE 125

1. ROSE SPRIG water pitcher, relish dish, tumbler.
2. ACORN goblet, butter dish (cover missing), bowl of sauce dish.
3. PRESSED LEAF water pitcher, goblet, spoonholder, footed salt.
4. ACORN VARIANTS goblet, goblet with leaf panel, creamer, water pitcher.

PLATE 126

1. DAHLIA creamer, water pitcher, cordial, footed sauce dish.
2. LILY of the VALLEY sugar bowl, goblet, creamer, plain footed creamer.
3. WILDFLOWER water pitcher, creamer, wine, footed sauce dish.
4. WILDFLOWER celery vase, sugar bowl, tumbler, bowl.

PLATE 127

1. Elephant match holder, saddle match holder, covered salt with rooster medallion, dog's head as knob of cover.
2. Bird salt with cherry in beak, turtle WILDFLOWER salt, frog match holder.
3. Squirrel salt, Swan mustard jar, Bear jar, 4½ inch.
4. Owl creamer, rabbit covered dish, dog salt.

PLATE 128

1. BLEEDING HEART compote on high standard, creamer, butter dish.
2. BLEEDING HEART spoonholder, footed tumbler, tumbler, egg cup.
3. STIPPLED FORGET-ME-NOT cup and saucer, tumbler, oval salt, bowl of sauce dish.
4. STIPPLED FORGET-ME-NOT compote on high standard, water pitcher, celery vase.

PLATE 129—LARGE PLATES

Palmette   Willow Oak
Dahlia   Stippled Forget-Me-Not

PLATE 130—GOBLETS

Stippled Forget-Me-Not
Dahlia

Panelled Forget-Me-Not
Horseshoe or Good Luck

PLATE 131—LARGE PLATES

Horseshoe or Good Luck   Star Rosetted

Frosted Circle   Barred Forget-Me-Not

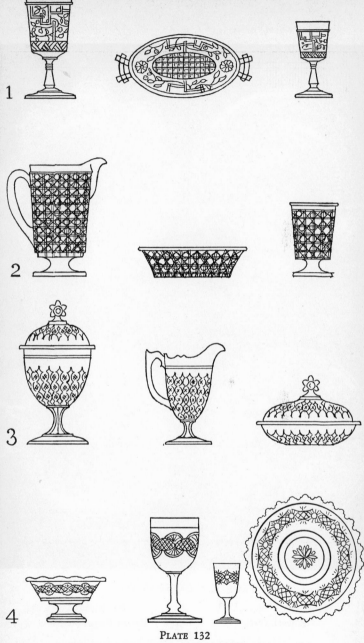

PLATE 132

1. BARRED FORGET-ME-NOT goblet, pickle dish, cordial.
2. CANE water pitcher, relish dish, spoonholder.
3. DOUBLE SPEAR sugar bowl, creamer, butter dish.
4. CHAIN footed sauce dish, goblet. CHAIN with STAR cordial, plate, 7 inch.

PLATE 133—BREAD PLATES

Horseshoe or Good Luck	Panelled Forget-Me-Not
Flower Pot	The Lord's Supper

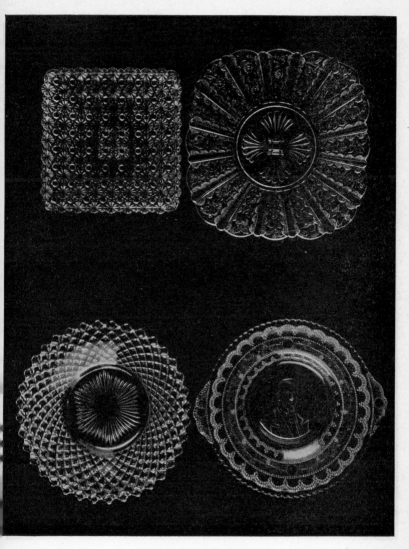

PLATE 134—PLATES

Daisy and Button   Panelled Daisy
English Hobnail   Odd seven inch plate

PLATE 135—SIX AND SEVEN INCH PLATES

Snakeskin

Princess Feather

Roman Rosette

PLATE 136

1. FLOWER POT sugar bowl, creamer, water pitcher.
2. STIPPLED WOODFLOWER sugar bowl, creamer.
3. PRIMROSE covered compote, creamer, goblet, footed sauce.
4. PANELLED DAISY celery vase, compote on high standard, goblet.

PLATE 137

1. RIBBED FORGET-ME-NOT sugar bowl, creamer, butter dish.
2. HEAVY JEWEL sugar bowl, creamer, butter dish, spoonholder.
3. THOUSAND EYE (three knob) celery vase, egg cup, compote.
4. THOUSAND EYE (plain) celery vase, water pitcher, bowl.

PLATE 138—SEVEN-INCH PLATES

Fine Cut   Stippled Forget-Me-Not
Diamond Cut with Leaf   Dahlia

PLATE 139

1. BARBERRY sugar bowl, pickle dish, spoonholder.
2. BARBERRY covered bowl, covered compote, footed sauce dish.
3. CURRANT sugar bowl, creamer, celery vase.
4. WINDFLOWER creamer, tumbler, spoonholder, egg cup, footed salt.

PLATE 140

1. SCROLL covered compote, sugar bowl, goblet, spoonholder.
2. THISTLE goblet, tumbler, spoonholder, egg cup.
3. SCROLL with FLOWERS creamer, goblet, egg cup.
4. DIAGONAL BAND creamer, goblet, water pitcher.

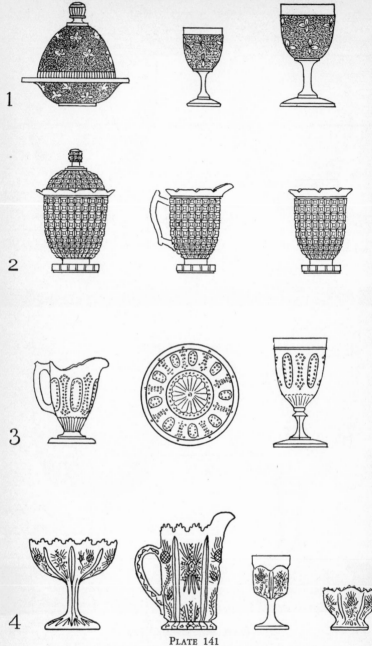

PLATE 141

1. STIPPLED CLOVER butter dish, cordial, goblet.
2. MILK-WHITE WAFFLE sugar bowl, creamer, spoonholder.
3. "101" creamer, plate, goblet.
4. PANELLED THISTLE compote, water pitcher, cordial, salt.

PLATE 142—GOBLETS

Blackberry   Currant
Strawberry   Barberry

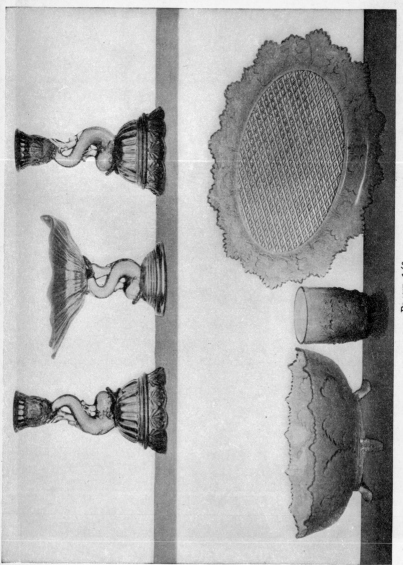

PLATE 143

PLATE 144—LARGE PLATES

Diamond Cut with Leaf   Odd Daisy bread plate

Grant Peace plate   Maple Leaf plate

PLATE 145—LARGE PLATES

Teasel

Festoon

Stippled Cherry

Ivy in Snow

PLATE 146—GOBLETS

Thousand Eye   Cathedral
    Swirl   Stippled Ivy

PLATE 147

1. RIBBED OPAL berry bowl, bowl of sauce dish, handled cup.
2. RIBBED OPAL creamer, pitcher, tall tumbler.
3. SPIRALLED IVY sugar bowl, spoonholder, water pitcher, tumbler.
4. STIPPLED STAR celery vase, base of sugar bowl, goblet.

PLATE 148—GOBLETS

Loop and Dart, diamond ornaments   Loop and Dart, round ornaments
Double Loop and Dart   Loop and Dart

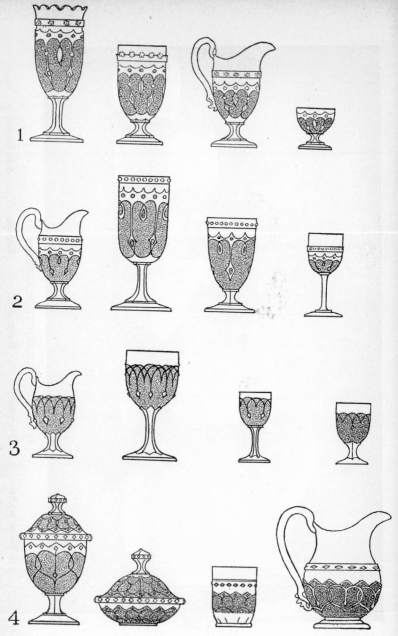

PLATE 149

1. LEAF and DART celery vase, footed tumbler, creamer, footed salt.
2. LOOP and DART (round ornaments) creamer, celery vase, footed tumbler, cordial.
3. LOOP and DART creamer, goblet, cordial, egg cup.
4. LOOP and DART (diamond ornaments) sugar bowl, butter dish, tumbler, water pitcher.

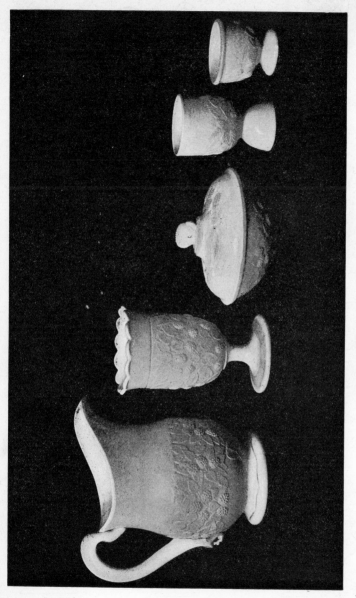

PLATE 150—MILK-WHITE BLACKBERRY

Water pitcher   Celery vase   Butter dish   Egg cup   Salt, footed

PLATE 151

1. STRAWBERRY and CURRANT goblet (showing both sides of bowl), butter dish.
2. LOGANBERRY and GRAPE goblet (showing both sides of bowl), water pitcher.
3. STRAWBERRY creamer, sugar bowl, spoonholder, egg cup.
4. BLACKBERRY celery vase, spoonholder, footed salt.

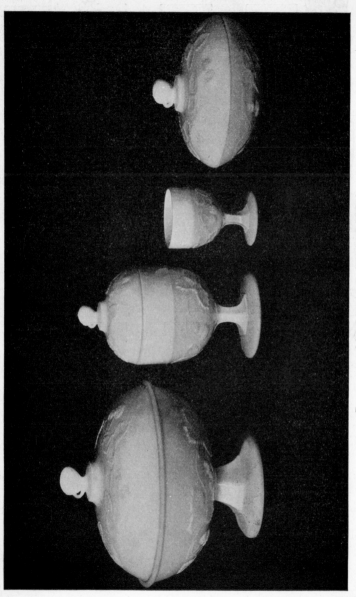

PLATE 152—MILK-WHITE STRAWBERRY

Covered compote   Sugar bowl   Egg cup   Butter dish

PLATE 153—GOBLETS
Including many odd patterns not collectible in other forms.

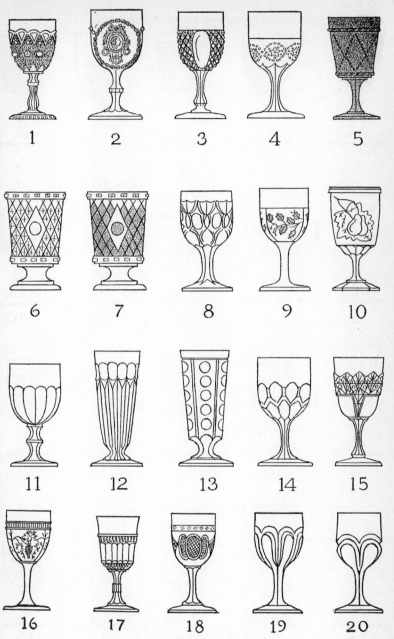

PLATE 154—GOBLETS
Including many odd patterns not collectible in other forms.

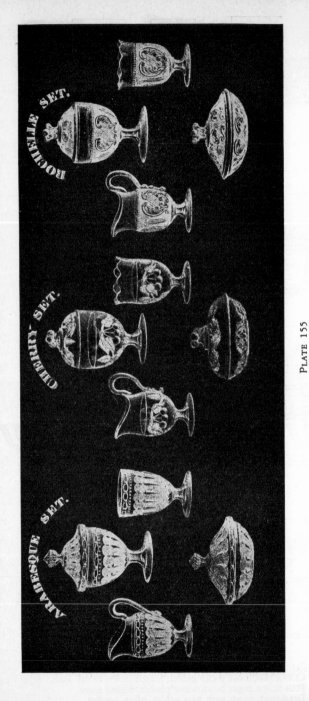

PLATE 155

Arabesque, Cherry and Rochelle (now termed Princess Feather) "sets," as taken from page of an old trade catalogue of Bakewell, Pears & Co.

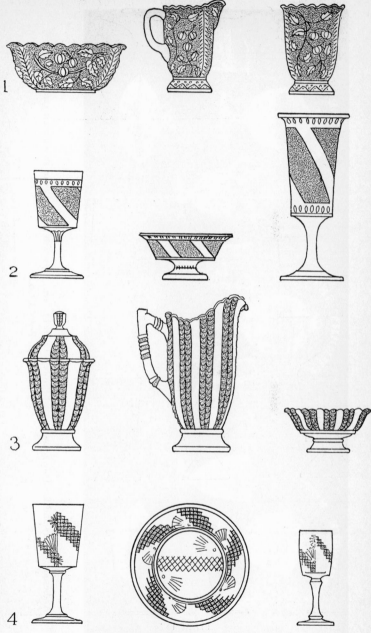

PLATE 156
1. STIPPLED CHERRY berry bowl, creamer, celery vase.
2. CLEAR DIAGONAL BAND goblet, footed sauce, celery vase.
3. FISH SCALE sugar bowl, water pitcher, footed sauce.
4. DIAGONAL BAND with FAN goblet, plate, cordial.

PLATE 157

1. SHELL and TASSEL (square) tray, cake plate on standard, covered compote, footed sauce dish.
2. SHELL and TASSEL (round) sugar bowl, butter dish, celery vase.
3. PLEAT and PANEL sugar bowl, creamer, spoonholder, footed sauce dish.
4. ROMAN ROSETTE sugar bowl, creamer, spoonholder, butter dish.

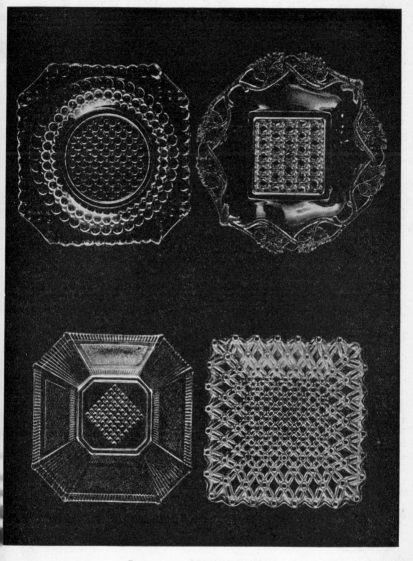

PLATE 158—SQUARE PLATES

Thousand-Eye   Maple Leaf, variant
Pleat and Panel   Nailhead

PLATE 159

1. MARQUISETTE goblet, compote on high foot, spoonholder.
2. WILLOW OAK water pitcher, creamer, goblet.
3. TWO-PANEL creamer, sugar bowl, celery vase.
4. THREE-PANEL celery vase, butter dish, creamer, footed sauce dish.

PLATE 160—GOBLETS

Two Panel   Fine Cut and Panel
Fine Cut   Cane

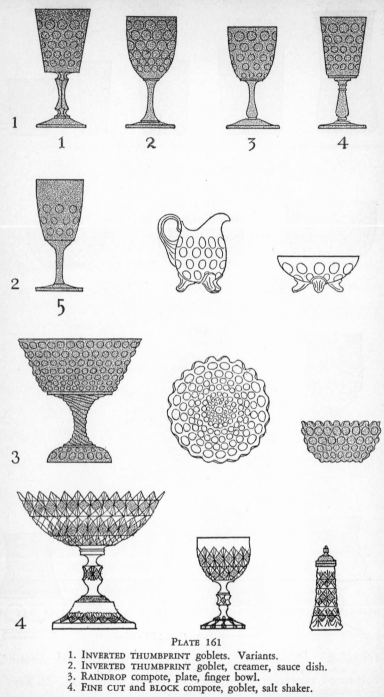

PLATE 161

1. INVERTED THUMBPRINT goblets. Variants.
2. INVERTED THUMBPRINT goblet, creamer, sauce dish.
3. RAINDROP compote, plate, finger bowl.
4. FINE CUT and BLOCK compote, goblet, salt shaker.

1. CRANBERRY RED INVERTED THUMBPRINT celery vase, small celery vase, tumbler, wine, punch cup.
2. INVERTED THUMBPRINT. Three varieties of finger bowls; large, with base; medium and small.
3. RED BLOCK goblet, sugar bowl, cordial.
4. RUBY THUMBPRINT goblet, spoonholder, pint pitcher, celery vase.

PLATE 163—PLATES

Ray   Swirl
Maple Leaf, variant   Daisy and Button

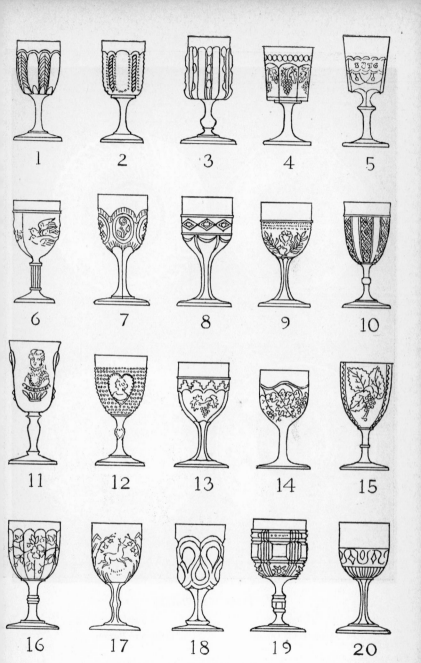

PLATE 164—GOBLETS
Including many odd patterns not collectible in other forms.

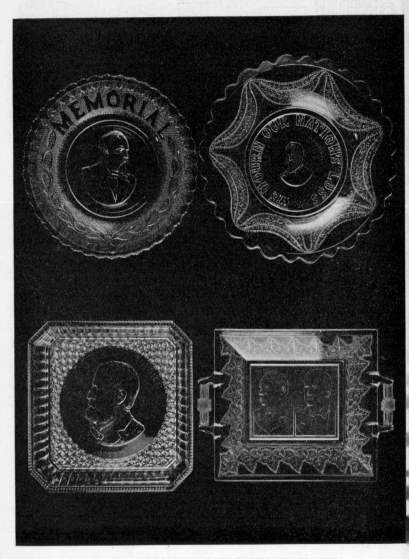

PLATE 165—MEMORIAL AND CAMPAIGN PLATES

| Garfield Memorial | Garfield Drape |
| Grant | Cleveland and Hendricks |

PLATE 166

1. SOUTHERN IVY water pitcher, bowl of sauce dish, berry bowl.
2. BUCKLE with STAR goblet, bowl of sauce dish, pickle dish.
3. FESTOON spoonholder, bowl of sauce dish, creamer.
4. GOOSEBERRY goblet, tumbler, spoonholder.

PLATE 167—GOBLETS

Variant of Daisy and Button with V ornament   Daisy and Button with cross bar

Daisy and Button   Daisy and Button with Thumbprint

PLATE 168—DAISY AND BUTTON TUMBLERS

With Thumbprint
Crossbar with Thumbprint

With V ornament
Crossbar with pointed ornaments

PLATE 169—DAISY AND BUTTON

PLATE 170—DAISY AND BUTTON

Crossbar celery vase   Butter dish   Creamer   Water pitcher
With Thumbprint, compote on high standard   Compote on low standard   Cake plate on standard

PLATE 171—DAISY AND BUTTON

PLATE 172—MILK-WHITE WHEAT PATTERN COMPOTE AND BUTTER DISH

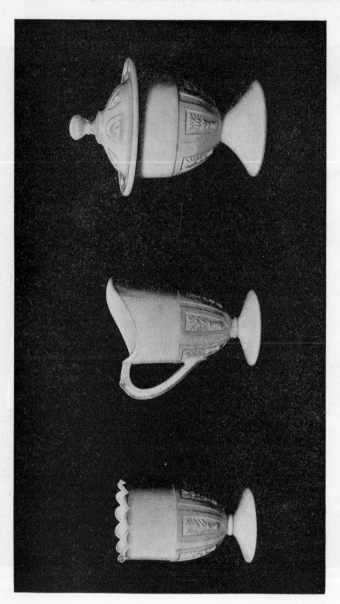

PLATE 173—MILK-WHITE WHEAT PATTERN SPOONHOLDER, CREAMER AND SUGAR BOWL

PLATE 174—MILK-WHITE PLATES AND FISH PLATTERS

PLATE 175—MILK-WHITE "LACE EDGED" BOWLS

PLATE 176—LARGE PLATES

Lattice edge in milk-white   Open edge in Marble glass

Milk-white plate with Gothic border

PLATE 177

MILK-WHITE VASES IN ROSE PATTERN   GOBLET AND PLATE IN OPAQUE CREAM COLOR

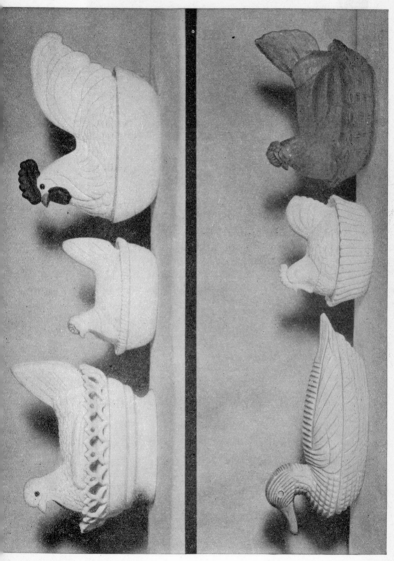

PLATE 178—MILK-WHITE COVERED DISHES

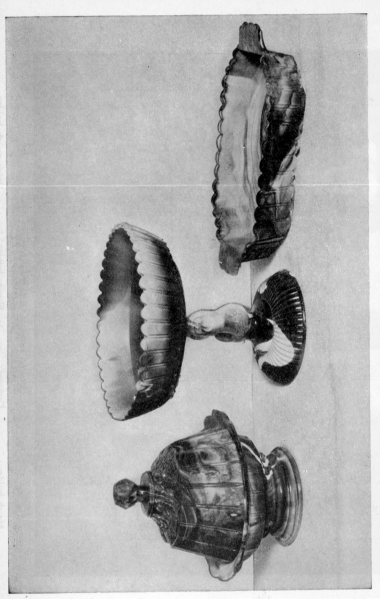

PLATE 179—MARBLE GLASS IN FLUTED PATTERN

Butter dish   Compote   Oblong deep dish

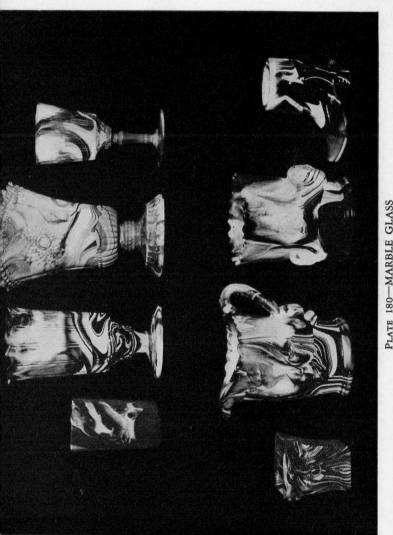

PLATE 180—MARBLE GLASS

Tumbler   Celery vase   Vase   Goblet

Match holder   Creamer   Flower holder   Boot match holder

(Creamer and flower holder in yellow and white marbleized glass)

PLATE 181

1. MILK-WHITE covered melon dish, SWAN salt, covered melon dish.
2. MILK-WHITE eagle covered dish, hen lace-edged covered dish, GRAPE salt.
3. Cow mustard jar, hen covered dish, log cabin.
4. OPAQUE BLUE OWL, yellow and white MARBLE glass flower holder, FISH covered dish.

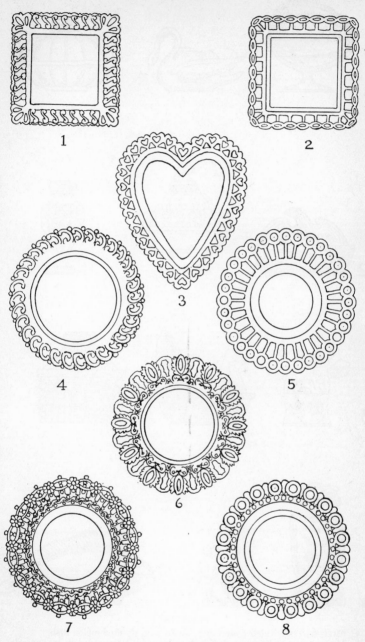

1   2

3

4   5

6

7   8

PLATE 182—MILK-WHITE PLATES

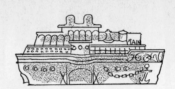

1

2

3

4

PLATE 183

1. MILK-WHITE tall eagle inscribed "E Pluribus Unum"; battleship Maine, small covered hen dish.
2. MILK-WHITE dish with fish on cover, dish with turtle on cover.
3. MILK-WHITE sleigh with hen on cover, dish with lion on cover.
4. MILK-WHITE battleship with Uncle Sam on cover, dish with head of Admiral Dewey on cover.

PLATE 184

Page from Bakewell, Pears & Co. catalogue illustrating their opaque "Rochelle" pattern. This is now known as Princess Feather.

PLATE 185—KNIGHTS OF LABOR PLATTER

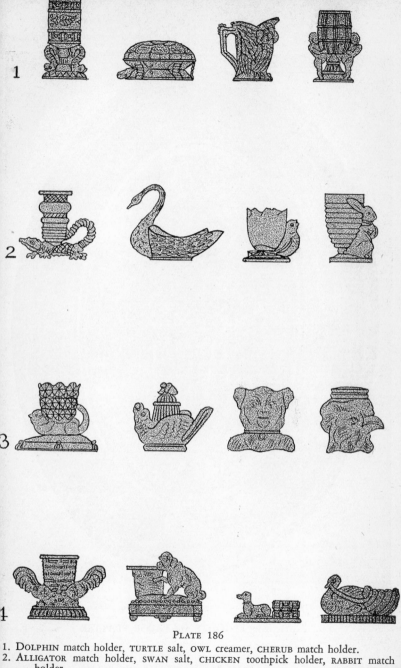

PLATE 186

1. **DOLPHIN** match holder, **TURTLE** salt, **OWL** creamer, **CHERUB** match holder.
2. **ALLIGATOR** match holder, **SWAN** salt, **CHICKEN** toothpick holder, **RABBIT** match holder.
3. **KITTEN** match holder, **BIRD** mustard jar, **MONKEY** toothpick holder, **ROOSTER** salt.
4. **ROOSTER** match holder, **DOG** match holder, **DOG** salt, **SWAN** salt.

PLATE 187—LARGE PLATES

Late Thistle   Block with fan border

Open edge, with basket weave center   Double Vine

PLATE 188
DEEP DISH WITH SHEAF OF WHEAT IN CENTER
LARGE TRAY WITH SCENE DEPICTING NIAGARA FALLS

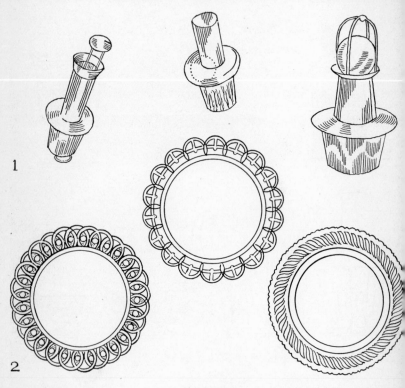

PLATE 189
PATENT CORKS
MILK-WHITE PLATES

PLATE 190—ODDS AND ENDS

INDEX

Index

Index

Index

Index

Index

Index

Index

Index

Index